CANARY IN THE DARK

A collection of poems

Bruce Colbert

CANARY IN THE DARK
Copyright ©2021 Bruce Colbert
Cover Photo- Lewis Hines

All rights reserved. Blue Jade Press, LLC retains the right to reprint this book. Permission to reprint poems from this collection must be obtained by the author.

ISBN- 978-1-7374758-0-4

Published by:

Blue Jade Press, LLC

Blue Jade Press, LLC
Vineland, NJ 08360
www.bluejadepress.com

For my grandfather Thomas Davis, born South Wales, 1894

Though lovers be lost love shall not.
-- Dylan Thomas

Table of Contents

Light Across the Roof	1
Drunken Breath	2
Checkered Past	4
Sickly Sweet Smell	7
Dark Brown Eyes	8
Abandoned Breaker	10
Death Knell	12
Slag Pile Summers	14
Dutchman	17
Canary in the Dark	18
Hungry Fire	20
Truth Worn Bible	22
Climbing to that Upstairs Bathroom	23
Perfume of an Industry	25
Blown Hole	26
Stale Afternoon	28
Wet Boots, Cold Beer	29
Belgrade Street Corner	31
Rising Dawn	33
Against these Same Hillsides	34
Lush Green Grass	35
Circuit Rider	38
Cotton Dress with Smart Sandals	40
Flotsam in the Stinging Surf	42

Part Two: Walking on Wet Streets

Company of Sharks	45
Requiem in B Minor	47
Bodhisattva	49
Fast Train Oblivion	51
Stray Alley	54
Warmer Still Water	55
Outside these Dotted Lines	57

Without a Destination	58
Third Floor Front	60
Marais	62
Dollar at a Time	63
When the Beginning Sadly Becomes the End	65
Before Eight o'clock Mass	67
Sinai	68
Walking on Wet Streets	69
Try to Remember	70
Troubadour	72
Writ Large	73
Frangipani	74
Refused Asylum	75
Mazurkas	77
Piney Woods	78
Sparrows	79
Trigger Finger	80
Anonymous Rain	81
Unvarnished	82
Summer of a Very Small Discontent	84
Crumbling Ramparts	85
Alto Saxophone Notes	86
Undisciplined Pelicans Fly South	88
Night Talk	90
Unwelcome	91

Light Across the Roof

He kept me afraid for as long as I was around, my father and this same fear made me become invisible to him, the only reason for any normalcy in our crowded home.

When he left for some assignment the army sent him on, usually months, sometimes years, she would sit alone in the living room, not lonely I believed, but somehow happy that he'd gone.

Absence of any love from him drove her deeper into a depression she'd already had for her whole life, and at thirteen coming into the tiny apartment above a shoe store on the town's main street that summer evening

I'd see the glowing cigarette ember like a beacon in the darkness, shouting in its way to all those ships in the uncharted sea, and somehow I was one too broken below the water line.

It warned, stay away from the perilous shoals of this doomed household, flee and quickly.

With a glance, and a word or two, usually unanswered, I swerved down the narrow hallway to the boxy space and this gunmetal

Battered army cot that sat in my room, and used the light from the neighbor's bedroom window across the tarred roof as a safe passage into the black night.

Drunken Breath

I learned about cruelty at an early age, wary of those hard boot footsteps of my Army sergeant father, afraid of his few acidic and piercing words to me, if he spoke at all, usually calling me, "You."

As if he were speaking to a common soldier who couldn't find his courage in the muddy trenches,

Whom he would beat into some act of sacrifice, or even madness, with no avowed purpose as history would later prove.

Stinging hindsight of a now certainty.

He was often gone and would send us back to the coal town where he and my mother had lived as children,

Generally, to the succor of her parents' home, or to one of the few apartments on the commercial street with the two-story department store Bright's,

But it was escape nevertheless, almost as if with metal file and shovel I'd broken out of some stone walled and barred prison, eluding the somnolent tower guards.

When my consciousness of a young boy began at ten, I dreamt of how I might kill him albeit painlessly, and

So it became those thoughts that occupy a young mind before sleep, and that part of the man he would later become,

Though the gentleness I had learned from those pious Welsh grandparents made this death wish unrequited even in those boyhood fantasies of toy soldiers and plastic pistols, and

In truth I really only wanted him to love me, which it never seemed he could, yet his distance and arrogance seemed close to abating when I became a man

Married with a child of my own, a daughter, and his last drunken breath of dismissal was the legacy finally left me.

Checkered Past

When I had started high school in a sagging stone battleship of a building that housed grades one through twelve, the

Coal mines in the Panther Valley had begun their final death rattle,

At least four or five mines were shuttered the year I returned for ninth grade as my parents decided to separate with my father remaining on the army base in Virginia while my mother,

Myself and my sister looked for an apartment large enough to house a family of three, and found one on Ridge Street near the Amvets above a lumber and hardware store.

As a twelve-year-old, I'd remembered that my grandfather's younger miner friends, some a generation or more behind him, had been laid off from the three mines outside Nesquehoning.

A surplus food center had opened in town where they gave people out of work bricks of cheddar cheese, powdered milk and canned pork, those three items, that's all.

When I visited my grandparents the log of orange cheese would be sitting on the kitchen table,

And if I went two doors over to Strauss' Bar to get a quart of root beer they liked I noticed the same cheese perched on the stained wooden bar for customers to make sandwiches.

It seemed that everyone in town had started eating more cheese, though the beer drinking continued as before.

In those days, you could get a six-ounce draft beer for a dime, so even an unemployed miner could sit on a bar stool for an hour with only a dollar in this pocket, and maybe forget his misery. Though I doubt they did.

There'd be night baseball on the bar television in summer, but there could as easily have been Lawrence Welk and his bubbly champagne music too.

Most everyone was polite, and you'd always hear laughter amidst the complaints. This was a place where you had to tighten your belt sometimes. That was the way it was, had been forever.

By then, this was 1960, the United Mine Workers Union itself was dead broke after fifty years of corruption, and who was to blame?

A miner's pension check came for maybe eight months like my grandfather's did and suddenly it stopped forever. He told me that at the kitchen table once, wanted to curse but didn't. Instead he poured himself another beer from the brown quart bottle.

These men could pick slate out of the coal piles as they had as boys, but the mines were finished.

The next year four more deep mine shafts closed, and by the time I left high school only one was left when there had been eleven pouring out tons of coal at the end of the Second World War.

It was similar to waking up after a long strenuous and wonderful Saturday afternoon playing softball,

Some letter in the mail said you had cancer, the kind where there wasn't a cure like leukemia. And you can't cut out all the blood.

That year I joined the Navy the town was still breathing yet when I came back three years later it seemed that everyone on the streets was grasping for the air of a forgotten past.

A few more children's clothing factories had sprung up for miners' wives to sit at sweat shop-like sewing machines,

Maybe with more coffee breaks but with only minimum wages, and those more responsible men who weren't drunk every night on their misery hit the highways for Allentown an hour away or for a factory somewhere in New Jersey.

Finally, the town began to slowly choke on its own dusty breath. It would take another ten or even fifteen years to finish off the corpse that I knew so well as a boy.

Sickly Sweet Smell

For years afterward the scent of men's cologne in a room, an office, a restaurant, to me was like the coal gas that killed shaft miners,

It wasn't odorless true, instead it was a sickly sweet smell like some rotting gardenia past its bloom, brown and dead

Reminders of the moment I knew my father had entered a room, almost like a startled deer senses danger in the acrid wind, a warning to escape if escape were even possible, which it usually wasn't.

It's strange how nearly sixty years later I can walk into a room in New York, or Chicago, or almost anywhere, and that furtive alarm,

That sense of danger fills my nostrils, and two thoughts cloud my mind in that instant, stay to fight, or flee,

And I force a hard smile with this same remembrance, knowing that the lesson of the pack has never deserted me, and I don't turn knowing the attacker is imagination.

In that moment, I'm again a reconnaissance trooper sand covering my fingers and mapping escape.

Flies are in my eyes but it doesn't matter, I want this to be over.

Dark Brown Eyes

I was a Navy ensign commissioned two or three months when I heard that my mother's cousin's son was a marine on the same base,

So I felt compelled from the usual family obligations to at least see him. I hadn't seen him since he was a toddler.

I had always adored his mother who had paid attention to me as a small boy. I made a few calls to find him.

Left a message at his barracks and he called me back, and we arranged to meet the next night at a pizza restaurant outside the main gate, along the strip of fast-food joints and bars that served the sailors and marines.

There were a few young women on the streets, not many, mostly the cadres of twenty-year old men with shaved heads,

Swinging their arms in silent cadence as they walked the two or three anonymous blocks.

Inside a booth we ordered a large pizza and a couple beers, and he talked, told me about how he hated the brutal stepfather he'd inherited, and how he had to join the marines before he went crazy.

His mother became this man's property, something he owned like a dog, and beat when it amused him.

Resenting and ignoring him and his older sister. His words were harsh, and pained.

He was a handsome and fierce young man whose teenage years had been flattened with the hammer of hatred,

And I started to offer something, but I could see he wanted nothing I sought to give him.

And within an hour we had said what we were meant to say to each other, and we left the restaurant.

He gave me a firm handshake and I told him we must do this again to which he gave a slight unconvinced nod.

With that, we walked in separate directions.

A year or maybe two later, I learned that he had been found dead on a North Carolina beach face-down in the sand, a bullet hole in the back of his head.

And as the years flew by the crime went unsolved, and I mourned the dark-haired young man who had my mother's and her cousin's dark eyes I remembered, that almost black color.

Abandoned Breaker

Except for acres of pine trees planted by the high school class of '43 off the highway to Lehighton and outside the valleys of Pennsylvania Dutch farms,

Most of the hills had been scraped clean covered with black slag from the half dozen mines.

Right before you got to the pine forest sat an abandoned coal breaker with its long conveyor neck extending into the black earth like a feeding goose.

At dark it had the appearance from the road of a prehistoric mammal.

And you half expected it to shriek out painfully in the night air like the wounded animal it was.

Stillness replaced these steam whistles that for maybe eight years had announced the shift change in the mine,

Or at solemn moments a mining disaster, some explosion, or cave-in down inside the deep shaft.

For a time after the mine was shut, wintertime brought snowballs aimed at the few glass windows two stories above, with only a few broken thanks mostly to the lack of pubescent sharpshooters.

These were boys who would never take the cage down into the pits, instead they'd mine jungles in Asia with low slung carbines.

An anthracite mine emptied of old men, grandfathers and gaunt grey-temple fathers with grown sons and daughters,

And it washed away this bitter detritus into the frame house living rooms and bars with folded callus hands and desperate hopes.

They'd never be a real museum to what passed, only a broken and battered landscape left to ruin and the ashen sky.

Death Knell

By the time I was a boy no one that I knew was sending their brothers or sons down into the mines.

The Korean War and heating oil had given anthracite coal the knockout punch so many families had pretended didn't happen, but it did.

After the first round of layoffs, I can remember my grandfather as fire boss at the Number 11 mine five miles outside of town had heard the rumors of its closing as

Had most of the miners there. And those winter months when he came home after cleaning up in the wash shanty,

That desolate brick building, he would talk to my grandmother about it in a whisper in the kitchen but the tone was ominous and then

The dreaded day finally came when the Lehigh Coal and Navigation company announced the mine would be closed until further notice, and

It wasn't even some adjusting of the bottom line from red to black.

It was a hemorrhage, certain death of the broken jagged coal face, and the way of life the five towns in this overworked valley had known, almost forever, even before the civil war, at the beginning of steam power.

Men and women too would talk about it shaking their heads on the street, in the backyards under clotheslines,

On the way down the steps of church after the Sunday services, Catholic and Protestant stone faced.

But this was different. It was the disappearance into oblivion, erasing all memory of a hundred years, gone with a single cataclysmic explosion of a pen.

And for the next twenty-five years the survivors of this barren stained landscape would stagger shell-shocked through lives not unfamiliar with want but now of any hope.

Slag Pile Summers

Maybe three of us, boys, climbed the mountain without a name closest to the town, a mountain with trees and rocks that had no coal,

This Appalachian hump against the blue sky, and ran through the waist-high blueberry bushes grabbing handfuls on the way down the other side, finding a dusty trail that others had taken before us,

The summer sun hot on our bare necks, carrying the cheapest fishing rods we could find, borrowed, bought in the back of the hardware store,

Or in the crowded alcove of the Five and Ten Cents store, something the clerk called, "Sporting stuff," you see just before you went down three wooden steps and out the back door.

On the way down the mountain you could see the glassy lake, dark green in the afternoon light, and then on the horizon another rounded peak reclined with its drinking water reservoir hidden among the oak and maple hardwoods.

And on both sides as you stood above the town encircled by low lying black hills of coal slag

And the three or four breakers near the shafts you saw the Coaldale mine and in the opposite direction two more along the range toward Jim Thorpe, and the railroad terminus.

That's where the mining company sent the coal cars south to Philadelphia, or east toward New York.

Where passengers came by train to the valley towns, this single story brick terminal with four or five hard benches inside.

Before you got to the lake and the large electrical power plant for the valley, there was a lily pad pond covered called Tippet's, and for seventy-five cents, they'd rent a rowboat for as many hours as you could stand the hot sun,

And you'd fish for Brim, or Suns, and maybe Bass, but I never knew anyone who'd caught a Bass,

Only talk, even from the few men who came once in a while, retired miners.

There'd always be a few lost souls on the pond, older men who rarely spoke, and just stared at their line in the water. And they always put their scarred callused finger up to the mouths, and whispered for us to be quiet.

"You'll scare the fish," they hissed across the water. But you always got something, each trip.

You had a metal stringer for the fish you caught, usually three or four about the size of your hand, and hooked them through the gills, and you tied them onto your belt loop on the way back.

The way back was longer, more tiring and maybe it turned a little dark on the way down the mountain.

You could see the lights in the town, and the three story coal breakers out of the darkness, full of smoke and turmoil, with black slag spewing out their mouths onto some enormous pile. We didn't think much about the mines then.

By the time I was ten or twelve we'd been warned off mining, the danger, the layoffs and the whole foul industry.

We'd seen our miner grandfathers raspy and choking on the frame house back porches with oxygen tanks on their way to a slow smothering death.

I'd visited Johnny Williams with my grandfather in the hospital, and he was past the help of an oxygen tank, maybe fifty-seven or so, and he'd be suffocated by black lung three months after we left his bedside.

He and Charley Hand and the others had mined since they were teenagers, cracked the coal face in a half dozen mines alongside my grandfather.

Dutchman

When the tall big handed Dutchman two houses down from my grandparents died, I said something about how much I had always liked that man.

Like other young miners before the war he'd signed up and fought with the Marines in Okinawa I had remembered hearing. He'd been in my mother's high school class, liked her and the family.

Someone, I can hardly recall who it might have been, stopped me when I told him I'd miss Ralph.

And they laughed, this old man whomever he was, and he said, "You probably didn't know what Ralph did, for your mother."

"What?" I asked, and he leaned over and in a faint voice said, "Your father wouldn't give your mother any child support, wouldn't help out at all. That first time.

Ralph drove down to where he was staying and outside some bar gave him the worst beating of his life with those fists that hung around a mine pick nine hours a day, and

He told him as he left him on the sidewalk, "If you don't send Beth money for the boy, I'm coming back for you."

During all those years I had never known, and I patted the pensioner who told me the story on the shoulder,

And said, "I never knew why I liked Ralph so much," and a sad look crossed my face.

Canary in the Dark

In Lansford where we lived, the richest of the coal veins had been found a hundred years before I was born,

And at Number 9 mine a tunnel had been driven a mile into Sharp Mountain where the coal started,

And after the first face was harvested, the next level, or lift was dug down a few hundred feet, and another tunnel created.

You had boilers to create steam power at the head of the slope to pump out the water, and pump in the air for the miners cracking the seam.

Coal was worked on both sides of the gangway deeper and deeper each day from escape.

Inside these narrow corridors, timbers kept a ceiling from caving in, and with each crack of the pick you might open a cache of methane gas.

The horror of death was always there, nearby, silently waiting. Odorless. Unseen.

There had been disasters, and accidents, and deaths, and most miners didn't think about it much, they kept working, this living.

Decent wages, a wood frame company house.

When my grandfather went down into the pits as a boy of twelve in Wales, they used a canary in the dark.

Carried them in wooden cages as they walked the dim tunnels. And if the bird showed distress, and even died, it still gave you enough time to flee the gas.

Walking amidst the scurrying rats and the fetid damp, carbide miner's headlamp lights his small booted steps. 5:00am.

Even as an old man he'd never forgotten his boyhood avian charges from the Welsh coal fields and in those early mornings after he'd had his sweet tea,

You could hear him whistle together with the caged yellow bird in the warm green floored linoleum kitchen.

Hungry Fire

Your coal was usually delivered on humid summer days or the very early fall by one of the dump trucks the bald burly brothers drove around the valley towns,

And when they got too sick to continue the deliveries, their sons Donny and Lenny took over, dusty carbon copies of the older men.

Same smiles and stories for sullen coughing miners waiting on their wind-swept front porches.

Pea coal, newly-cracked from unwieldy slabs into marble-sized pieces at the colliery.

A black shard, razor edges where the fissures break, cuts your hands or face.

Family car would be removed from the street in front of the houses and the cellar window opened.

Sometimes you'd put a kitchen chair in the vacant parking space, letting everyone know it was coal delivery day.

But that was unusual, people seemed to know this somehow, an unspoken announcement on East Berstch Street.

When the heavy dump truck got there, the brothers would turn it perpendicular to the curb and back it up to fifteen feet toward the open narrow window below the brick house front.

They'd raise the truck bed with its hydraulics up to maybe a forty-five-degree angle,

And then they'd jump out of the cab and get a stainless steel coal chute and slide it into the narrow cellar window.

They'd attach the chute onto two hooks on the bed next to a small truck door and crank it open and the coal would slide down through the window into our bin.

Glistening petroleum sediment rocks in this Northeastern sunshine, washed, black hexagonal diamonds.

Smooth, glassy and Paleolithic. With empty chute moist and silvery.

You'd buy a ton of coal for the Pennsylvania winter months, and that would warm a three story wood frame house from a single furnace heating water into steam for radiators on the ground level and upstairs in the bedrooms and single bathroom.

Every day right after Thanksgiving my grandfather would throw a shovelful of this coal from the bin into the already burning furnace in the morning and one at night.

As I turned ten, he let me stoke the furnace, turn a crank to let the ash fall into a pan below the embers, and walk the five steps to the bin and fill a shovel, throwing the coal with a grunt on the hungry fire.

Truth Worn Bible

They came from the Rhondda in the 1840s, this small-statured Druidic tribe that spawned me, and Christian, built a wood frame Welsh Congregational church up on Abbott Street in the 1850s,

Sang familiar miner's hymns and listened half-distractedly with pit exhaustion to the fundamentalist at the front of the room, worn-bible truths, before the Civil War.

With an incomprehensible tongue of lyric consonants, Celtic, dying already in its utterance, mostly forgotten. And these work-tired men

Survived the Number 9 mine fire lit under Lansford and up into Summit Hill, burned for days, weeks, suffocating smoke. But no deaths, this time.

Fire in some shafts from the bitter winter of 1859 until 1910. Abandoned, roast this rich earthly crust.

Portal of imagined fallen angels, Lucifer's distinctive laugh in this abysmal darkness, but who can hear?

Later these same diminutive Welshmen and their round wives built a brick church on the main commercial street.

Called the First Baptist Church. Choir loft and a baptismal behind the simple altar. Absence of Episcopal vestments.

Salvation found within this lead piped River Jordan, apostle hands, this church with stiff-backed unfriendly pews and

Few flowers, whose inner darkness was illuminated through saintly stained-class scriptures and righteousness.

Climbing to that Upstairs Bathroom

Upstairs in that creaking floor bathroom, lone-paned window overlooking the clotheslines and grassy patch quilt backyards of other miners,

I still see my grandfather's straight razor in its stiff leather on top of the medicine cabinet right next to his dried horse bristle brush.

The razor that my mother had used to cut her wrists, drowning in that despondency of what her life had become, and perhaps long before.

She'd taken the gleaming steel blade that he kept sharp on a fearsome leather strop, and ran it over one of her thin wrists,

Drawing a line of final escape, a road not rutted deep enough for her death,

But that silent scream of agony, and sat quietly as was her way on the closed toilet seat, and watched the birds in the trees outside until she was found.

She didn't lose much blood as the cuts were shallow, and one of the town's doctors came quickly with the summons, and dressed the wounds.

I was twelve when it happened, and my mother was only thirty-two, and

Now so many years later I can hardly remember when I was thirty-two,

Except that it was full of heady days and nights, and a wife and child,

And the singular ambition of career, or at least the perception of those misaligned thoughts, the rightness.

So strangely to me, he continued to use the razor she'd held in her small womanly hands, and shaved maybe every other day,

Lathering his square face, and stropping the blade on the stained leather.

Now his age, in whatever autumn years have played out, it seems such an unsettling thought that he could hold that instrument of such pain in his hands again, yet he did.

The first time I opened the straight razor as a boy as a curiosity, it struck me not as a shaving instrument but rather some bayonet or scimitar of battlefield carnage.

I felt with its weight in my hand, that it could and would indeed kill, and it terrified me.

Perfume of an Industry

Below this choked mining town toward those mansard roof offices of the Lehigh Navigation and Coal company, this disappeared Caesar with half its offices lit

Meandered a narrow-bedded rock-strewn stream, bastard child of cold-water mountain spring parents and virginal snow run-off, though it wasn't;

A concrete bridge led the windy asphalt road toward the coal company offices, and down its sod banks we slid, a gaggle of boys.

Alum Creek, who had christened you so? Perverse offspring of perhaps raw Aluminum wastes,

Or maybe white-flecked lime from two or even ten mine-runoffs, swimming among the hares and mine rats and summer's sonorous Blue Jays.

No signs to warn of outward danger but industry's fetid perfume, and we'd sit along these sloped banks with our baseball cards and peanut butter sandwiches,

Watching the stained toilet paper and feces, laughing aloud as a rogue condom swam stealthy as an eel between the lichened rocks.

Blown Hole

I was six staying with my grandparents when there was an explosion early one morning at the Number 11 mine where my grandfather was employed as a foreman and Fire Boss. He worked there ten years.

That meant that at 5 o'clock each morning he and several other men inspected the various mining slopes

For fire, or the appearance of coal gas, and signaled an all-clear that it was safe for the miners to work the various vein faces.

Around ten, a planned demolition, fire in the hole, had somehow gone askew, and it sent a wall of coal in the opposite direction, with the lethal barrage of rock flying at the men standing in wait;

Several men including my grandfather had been hit in the arms and legs with shards. No one fatally it happened.

And the men were dressed in the wash shanty and sent home to recuperate. A doctor had examined them, and with a nurse had bandaged the injured.

He had come home with his hands cut and bandaged and a slice across his cheek colored a light blue from the obsidian rock splinters.

We were all worried but he remained silent and had his usual tea, and sat alone in the living room through the next day.

But a piece of the coal that hit his temple had started to become infected, and it needed attention.

So he called the general practitioner who came around and looked at it. And told him, that he needed to remove an embedded piece of coal.

Could he come around to his office, and he'd give him some anesthesia to deaden the pain and cut it out? It was a flake like a snipped fingernail, that's all.

"You're here now, do it," my grandfather told him, and the doctor shook his head no, and added, "It'll be too painful."

"Go ahead, I've had worse," my grandfather told him at the kitchen table.

And so I watched the doctor from the dining room doorway take out his silver scalpel from a black leather bag,

Dab some alcohol and ointment from a tube on the wound, and in two or three tries dig out the coal. There was blood on a rag he held.

Throughout the whole thing, the was no change on the miner's face and he was sixty then; and

He had these strange stoic ways I couldn't understand, born of those pits from boyhood and the privation that came with them.

As the doctor scraped his temple bone I winced, and I thought for a second this man whom I known all my young life, had smiled at me for a second with a simple shrug of the shoulder.

Stale Afternoon

On weekends I'd wash the faded pea green 1953 Chevrolet outside the faux brick sided house, and though I'd soap it continuously,

Every time I hosed it off with a stream of fresh water, coal dust would seep down the sides of the doors from under the chrome trim.

'The dust was everywhere and in everything lurking quietly underneath the row houses in town built in the Teens, and

There were stories that in Coaldale the next town over by the Number 9 mine entrance and breaker,

People had gone downstairs to get the wash and found the whole basement had disappeared into a black hole, some abandoned shaft, gone forever into that darkness.

Or the basement might be scalding hot because fifty or a hundred feet below it, fires might have been burning for thirty years.

And even when I'd sit on the front porch summers with my grandfather who had outlived all his miner friends,

Buried them all, everyone, and when he'd turned ninety and had been out of the mines for thirty years,

He could still spit up coal dust onto the handkerchief he kept in his pocket.

Wet Boots, Cold Beer

The American Legion downtown sat anchored on Ridge Street across the street from the town Post Office with its basement youth center,

Some half-hearted effort by teachers at the high school to do the right thing whatever that was.

It had a 50s jukebox, a ping pong table, a shuffleboard game, and a TV room.

You talked occasionally with a friendly girl, played a record or two and stood around, or maybe watched a western in the dark room by yourself.

When I came back on leave after the Navy and went with one of the Miller twins to drink at the Legion post it was nothing much of a place,

Just a bar with a row of stools, some Second World War framed photos, and a cadre of bad drinkers, most already half-drunk.

Self-destructive men who'd like to blame their war, or any American war for their sea of troubles. I knew one of the men,

I'd gone out with his divorced wife's younger sister, a baby-sitting date with ham sandwiches from another bar a block from their row house.

He vaguely recognized me, I was some image, somebody floating unnamed in his consciousness. We nodded acknowledgement, or at least I did.

One twin was a radar operator in the South China seas on a destroyer who had told me a story the time we were together in San

Francisco in some North Beach bar about how they had shot down one of our planes by mistake.

It had been forgotten, or covered-up, another blurb of friendly fire.

He told me afterward they changed commanding officers when they returned to homeport at Treasure Island, and nothing else was said.

There was one guy a year ahead of me in school who'd been kicked out of the Marine Corps for some reason,

Not with a dishonorable discharge, but something medical. He'd lost it during his basic training at Parris Island and he wasn't the only one. It happened.

Not everyone was ready for the abuse dished out by the DIs then.

It was Vietnam after all, and these sergeants wanted the grunts to know you'd be getting a lot worse from the Viet Cong.

They'd be shooting at you for real, no dummy ammo flying above your head. No hot showers. Roast beef.

We got our drinks, stood around and glanced at the last man's club glasses in the case behind the bar,

Where the last guy from the Second World War at the Lansford Legion would drink the bottle of champagne alongside the broken glasses. Those dead soldiers.

Harry Miller whispered to me this was goddamn stupid, these drunks drowning in nostalgia and the misplaced sentiment. So we drank up and walked out the door.

He died young I remembered, his brother always believed the Agent Orange had something to do with it.

Belgrade Street Corner

"People who are mean to animals, aren't nice people," this grandmother told her six-year-old granddaughter sitting next to her on the lurching L train car,

Coming out of the Adams and Wabash station in the Loop. Serbian I'd guessed by the heavy accent and the lined Balkan face, and she had probably seen some people in her time who'd willingly hurt both animals and humans in Kosovo.

Her bony index finger clothed in its cheap wool glove battered the stale nighttime train air as she spoke to the rapt child. His face Slavic too.

"You must always know that," she added, and silently looked out the window at the passing half-lit office windows, the train about to cross the murky Chicago River on its way north to Kimball.

And so, I tried to remember the night those many years ago, as my mother slept next to my eight-month old sister, and with the stealth he'd used in the Black Forest,

This man who slept with her on most nights, this father, came barging into the living room drunk, hitting a table, and waking the parakeet we'd bought to keep us company.

In this darkness with only the street light illuminating the small room, the bird began to cry out in alarm, its cage draped for sleep; And the man's anger was aroused, whose low cruel voice terrified this fragile family.

He walked over to the birdcage, tearing off the dish towel, and opened its tiny door as the bird flew frightfully from its wood perch, and then,

In a moment he grasped the shivering blue-feathered creature, and holding it tightly in one hand, breaking its neck with the other.

Rising Dawn

When most of us came back from Berlin or Guantanamo or Viet Nam or the South China seas, these coal villages we'd known sat mostly quieted,

Untended by human hands from when we left, moribund, and inhabited with this putative hopelessness or maybe simply the resolve to exist,

And you felt the herd had moved on, somewhere else. Left the footprints in the snow.

You might've been coming back from forty years before, from the Big Red One, so little had changed, and these sullen old men sitting on the porches had gotten older, that's all;
When you drove toward Tamaqua on the rutted resurfaced Route 309 maybe a mile outside of town, you'd see what was left,

That single mine to dig coal for the bitter valley winter, sending it somewhere else too, along the rail spur in front of the smoking colliery,

Painted this shade of light forest green perhaps with the misguided purpose that what the few men inside that mine were doing was somehow meant-to-be, life-affirming, and with this sulfurous smoke in the rising dawn.

Pawns. A pathetic handful of soul-ransomed Chevrolets in the chain link parking lot.

Were we any different? We screwed anonymously on those stained and sagging front seats of borrowed cars half-drunk on some abandoned colliery road desperate to invent some sense of being when in truth we had none.

Against these Same Hillsides

Walk this frigid battlefield. See its twisted death surrounding. Remember those silk unfurled flags,

As I've walked others: Shiloh on frosty Tennessee mornings with my young daughter alongside,

And crept through the Bastogne night as a friend drove us back from Brussels to Luxembourg.

Heard those same silenced voices. The anguish, and the corpses of, this defeated army lying opened-mouthed and black against these hillsides, the monuments of barb wire and,

Rotting boards and Keep Out signs that shutter the mine entrances. And these tormented disappeared souls, crying out for succor, or perhaps even some strange justice, heard only by this sharpened wind while,

The Pennsylvania snow freezes over rusted cables that brought coal up from the earth's bowels,

Now misspelled childish graffiti adorns that heavy oak mining company office door as those unsmiling broken panes give contested ground to this bitter cold.

Lush Green Grass

I was twelve the year they took my mother away to the state mental hospital, and to no one, not my grandparents, whose house I lived in,

Nor to my younger sister whom my grandparents said they couldn't look after, it was too much, and they were so old, not to anyone did I talk about it.

These same grandparents had known me well, I was the oldest of the grandchildren and I had stayed with them for holidays and summers, and

I thought much later that perhaps I'd become the stillborn son my grandmother lost in 1921. The two of us were different together somehow from the others.

The way we talked to each other, the ease with which we sat at the kitchen table and had tea, and laughed. And yet I was a boy.

I would sit and sip the hot tea and listen to her stories about growing up, the father she dearly loved, her brothers and sisters, and the other coal town people. It was never gossip, only stories, one after the other. Never vicious, or tragic.

My sister went back to the Virginia army base where my father was stationed as a soldier,

And he found a Methodist chaplain there who agreed to take her into his home for that year. She lived with the minister, and I didn't see her.

So my life became something else from what it had been, and I willingly went into the much safer world of that coal region and the kitchen and the brewed tea. It became something affirming I'd never known, and a refuge.

When we finally drove the hour away to the hospital for the first, and only visit for me,

I can still imagine those green lawns of the hospital grounds, and the stone benches for the patients to sit and breathe and listen to the bird songs and

Bask in the summer sunshine away from the electric shock treatments, the mind-numbing pacifying drugs, those unimaginable days and lonely nights.

My mother was sitting on a bench that we were directed to, and she had a friend there, a lawyer she said who was also a patient, and he was quite nice. But he excused himself in a moment, and left us.

My mother was so proud to have a lawyer as her friend, and I remember she lowered her voice, and

Told us that the poor man was always washing his hands, not in the water of the bathrooms,

But when he sat down at dinner, or breakfast, or even sitting on the bench with her. She felt so sorry for him, and his sickness.
The hospital seemed this monolith of stone buildings around me, this awful fortress at the time, dark and sinister, and I longed to get back into the car and flee.

This single visit was painfully short, we talked on the stone bench for a few minutes, and the four of us walked back to the building where my mother was staying,

And I remember we returned some card, or maybe a badge at the reception desk, and hugged her and said goodbye.
In the backseat, those manicured farms of the Lehigh Valley roamed past my eyes, and we started the long climb into the coal fields,

Crossing the Schuylkill River while all along the asphalt highway this boy's mind sought to erase a history as if it were a board game where no one lost.

Circuit Rider

My mother's first cousins were anointed in their coal town ways perhaps, and the youngest of the two,

A seminary Baptist, the more eccentric of the two men, occupied the pulpit in the church where the family had worshipped their whole lives, some fifty years.

Where we were all immersed in this Jordan's new world waters. Behind the altar.

Congregation of coal-miner widows, and the few self-righteous men who sat on those hard Sunday morning pews, somber, men of another time,

More circumscribed, and scriptural, far less forgiving, would-be Pharisees who acted as elders, dark-suited, frowning, and by the time he had ascended to this, literally all of these valley towns had become moribund, choking within their hopelessness and shuttered mines.

Collection plate offering that could hardly keep the building lights lit, and so he served as the shepherd of a different flock too, another Protestant denomination;

After that Baptist morning service, he drove the five miles with his missionary wife to Nesquehoning where he ascended to a Methodist pulpit in front a handful of the pious, and his wife Jean played the organ as she had earlier.

For his trouble, the Methodists gave him and his wife and two boys, the small frame house next to the church which had been its manse. And with this midnight blackened sleet hitting the aluminum siding, his ever loyal

Ecumenical wife detects the panoply of Handel's virtuosity in her dreams while he remembers the sound of sucking chest wounds from the soldiers who gripped his soft hands at the gate of heaven.

He didn't fit in here, his days as an Air Force chaplain otherworldly to these unresponsive ears, and he never would, and one day it had to end, and it did unpleasantly.

Cotton Dress with Smart Sandals

When my mother died I few out to Pennsylvania from the West Coast to empty out closets and hand over anything worth keeping to my sister,

Beyond the small probate cash in bank accounts, and spent one afternoon by myself in the ramshackle frame house. Of silent voices and those same odors.

Searching around in the attic I'd found her white wedding album, and I must have spent two hours staring at the photographs, and wondering,

Trying to imagine how these incongruous people had ever managed to find each other, and then attempt a marriage together.
Doomed from the beginning, as I had witnessed each month, and each year.

Never remembered my mother looking at those wedding pictures even once, safely hidden away in a cedar chest her own miner father had given her along with a few winter wool blankets, and this cheap cardboard

File of birth certificates and vaccination records, and those hand-tinted Easter portraits of my sister and me from Bright's department store.

A gold-lettered leather photo album with this uneven pile of fingered and discolored black and white prints stuffed into the plastic pocketed pages taken by someone who had mistakenly called themselves a photographer,

Long ago of these seemingly happy couples; those slicked-back hair grinning soldiers in tan army shirts with rows of campaign ribbons and sergeant stripes

Facing this summery half circle of Adirondack chairs with wasp waist young women

In cotton dresses and sandals sipping Tom Collins cocktails out of tall frosted glasses with red lipstick radiance, so incongruous, so impossible. These same people.

My mother is the only woman in the pictures not wearing sandals, hiding the toes on one foot which had been bent with polio when she was a child. Her short legs crossed and what she calls her crippled foot hidden in the shadow of the dress.

I quickly slipped the album into my office brief case, and started down the attic stairs, feeling such lingering pain in my heart that I had to walk a block or two before it left me though I knew it never would completely.

The empty sidewalk took me up the hill from the house to the shuttered pharmacy and across the street to what had been Botek's market and its sawdust floor,

Up the small hill to Charley Mullen's vacant barber shop where I'd gotten buzz haircuts for seventy-five cents and waiting had thumbed through Argosy and those other men's magazines he'd kept for the miners.

Composed, I had started back to the row house recognizing no one on the street, thirty or forty years or more vanished, and nearly half my high school class gone.

In time my daughter will make a similar thankless flight from Memphis to Chicago, or maybe the Alabama gulf coast, and
Sit in this stale air with death, and glance at an album of the two incongruous people she knew so well, somehow trying to interpret.

Flotsam in the Stinging Surf

When Viet Nam dumped its flotsam back in those coal valleys, little
had changed and not much attention was paid to the men

Who one-by-one got off the Trailways bus at Sharpe's News Agency
with a bag or two, maybe still in uniform with ribbons, unnoticed
really,

And they went quietly into the Rialto next door and used the phone
booth in the front of the restaurant to call someone at home to pick
them up.

A few had been killed but not those big numbers you'd see later;
This was a few years before Tet. Escalation of that selective
consciousness.

Someone from Summit Hill who used to hitchhike bare-chested all
summer to the shock or maybe delight, I can't remember, of the
women with children driving down to shop at Bright's Department
Store was one.

He'd been an Air Force security guard with a German Shepard dog,
patrolling along some deserted wire perimeter, and they both
disappeared in a dawn land-mine explosion. Arms and legs and
heart, all vanished.

What they found was sent back in some ceramic urn, or metal box
for burial. Died at a place called Hue, between that Imperial city
and Chu Lai.

In the two-room apartment on Ridge Street their sickly widower
father occupied above the Triangle shoe store, two brothers I'd
known

Got laboring jobs inside the forge at Bethlehem Steel, cleaning up
ingot spills, maybe in line for a union journeymen job,
though you needed to know someone who'd vouch for you, make a
call to a foreman, that's how it worked.

On the reel to reel tape recorder one of them had bought at the PX
in Nam, they played that song about John Henry, the steel-driving
man, each morning at four,

Threw some water on a sleepy boozy face, made some instant
Nescafe coffee, and piled into a beater car for the hour drive,
all the while laughing the way unconcerned young men do, never
quite certain of what card you'll be dealt though not caring. Never
the queen.

One of the now dead brothers had watched the jungle slough off the
vine then with a long seemingly happy marriage though childless
once told me, "Maybe I should've just grabbed one of those kids
that hung around. I don't have any."

Part Two

Walking on Wet Streets

Company of Sharks

Those two years I'd lived on the Sausalito sailboat were in the broadest sense almost accidental, the decision made within five minutes in a high-tension living room, painful, and final,

A suitcase and an entire life packed onto that white-hulled Catalina in one sunny afternoon; coming partly from an unfortunate

Misunderstanding about finding an apartment too near my separated spouse which had terrified her, this unsuspected

Surveillance I'd conjure up and put into practice, and after prolonged conversations with a shared therapist I'd relented, and the Princess Street apartment complex manager grudgingly returned a security deposit check I'd given him earlier in the week.

But not without making a scene, and threats. A banker friend had lived there.

Never a quite planned nautical address, sort of default I'd chosen somehow easier than those arguments, and I'd be acquitted, declared innocent. Of something sinister.

She'd met a man at an AA meeting she had wanted to be with in relative peace. We were mostly affable, and understanding people.

He was a man at least I had been friendly with, a guest for dinner on two occasions, the last when an out of town woman we'd known for years

Took me outside into the Rosemary hillside garden in the back, and said, "Can't you see what's going on?"

At the time, I told her that they were simply friends, and her imagination had gotten the better of her.

"It's right in front of you, my God," she said.

Then I remembered she grabbed me by the arms, squeezed hard, shook her head before hugging me, and we went back into the house as if the conversation hadn't occurred.

And of course I hadn't seen it, until later. But still it couldn't be saved.

I had simply agreed, and why not? I was that kind of man, uncertain.

The marriage had been leaking for maybe three or four years, and sinking to the bottom. I watched it go under and stood there, letting it happen.

Slowly this green Pacific bay and those creatures surrounding me in the air and under the sea changed me. Inside. Merlin gestures. These unfamiliar sounds and smells. Metaphysical and then finally magical. Moonlight and brackish water. Of mirrored sea serpents.

Aurora borealis on a shimmering plate. A darkness that wasn't darkness at all. With siren songs of softest wind. Through the open hatches.

Solitude a constant companion, and salvation, alone within this bosom of the night's silence amidst a company of sharks.

Requiem in B Minor

The grand piano sat as if it were a mahogany sea lion, wooden sail
raised to a broad reach on the perilous sea,

Undisputed master of its rocky terrain on a burnt orange Persian
rug, outside azaleas waved, pink blossomed.

First she played Mozart whom she adored, and on occasion Bach
like today which made her smile as her thin white fingers raced
tremolo across the ivory and black keys;

Her long blond hair hung down over these bluest eyes, hiding them,
though she knew the road this music took, knew its trodden paths,
its many turns;

Adagio of steamy southern afternoon hands that moved quickly as
the paintings of this woman and her sister glanced down from the
tangerine pale walls.

They approved, even without smiles that the painter had forbade.

Two children played quietly in the next room with toy cars and lacy
dressed dolls, and laughed to themselves as children do.
She stopped playing and put the sheet music into an embroidered
case on the piano bench, and smiled at her silver watch. It was time.

The black woman who looked after the children brought them
warm cookies and milk, and then the doorbell chime rang in its
familiar chorus.

This woman not yet thirty-five found her linen jacket in the hall
closet and saw the man outside from the picture window.

There was a husband naturally from a prominent family though he raised hunting dogs. Unconventional and too controlling. Monstrous, she had said after.

But there would be Episcopal cathedral schools and later Vanderbilt, or maybe Tulane, she didn't worry much, and

With a loud sigh she hugged her two small children, and rushed out the front door, leaving them forever.

I had once driven her and this deserted husband from that Civil War church wedding ceremony at LaGrange in someone's borrowed Lincoln Town car,

Married to her older sister, and remembered his nervousness kneeling at the altar.

His voiced had quavered as he said, "I take this woman," and he had tried to smile at his discomfort. And slowly he had found his way, and continued.

There was a boyish innocence that had made the small congregation uncomfortable particularly the older women, and maybe somehow they knew.

Bodhisattva

Determined not to leave me behind or lagging, her baseball cap
headlight singularly brighter in the mist of the predawn darkness,

Azimuth whose leather boots spoke first against hard clay paths and
then against the scattered gravel, spitting handfuls of

Pebbles with each grunted thrust of her hardened calves, skeletal
pistons to this mountain engine roar, and now silent into the
switchback, and back again, at once

Ascending to a somnolent lava field with even more stealth as her
woman's frame silhouettes the illuminated orange horizon, raven
hair goes akimbo,

Swung into the thin air as she takes off the peaked cap, and glances
back toward me with steeled tight furled smile
And then the nod of her head to continue, though faster, this pace
increased;

She will make me a Bodhisattva or perish, converted to a pristine
language of unsullied wilderness, this Himalayan cast at last mine.
Cairns of these Seven Noble Truths.

In the distance I watch the white and yellow Buddhist prayer flags
flutter on her backpack, and she disappears into a cedar and rock
canopy with a foot race that

I can barely manage, a small dark-haired woman who gives me no
quarter but as I climb higher the summit appears, and my heart
lightens toward the dormant

Volcano with chiseled basalt lips guarding the sculpted tree line, a
clown's greasepaint grin against those sad grey-faced Sierras,

Laughing through that narrow mountain pass down into the Oregon flatlands to the embrace of three loyal Sisters and the damp coastal Cascades, and into British Columbia.

At the odd-shaped fork below the summit completely exhausted with my shirt sticking to my back, I had noticed her Nepalese scarf tied to a branch pointing the way to my enlightenment.

For months we climbed and talked about those blurred lines between the spirit and physical worlds, heady wonderful excursions, and then later inhabited unfettered passion, though with time

Afterward we had the usual arguments between men and women, and those things we disliked about each other, those really small things, somehow became larger and one day too large for us.

She came into a restaurant during a business meeting once to make a scene, and I screamed at her on a downtown corner to my own embarrassment and the disapproval of a passing lunchtime suited army,

We retreated to separate mountaintops.

The end was painful and ugly, and I think we were both ashamed of it, because we were better.

Fast Train Oblivion

I had taken the L train from State and Lake downtown after visiting one of my oldest friends who had this prolonged hospital incarceration to get his breathing right, and

It had been an excruciating process for him, deathly. He'd seen the white light twice.

As the train groaned and jumped and started it made me think of his life, and mine too, we went back thirty-five years, through

Some of the rowdiest and also the most wonderful of times, those years, drinking those full measures of work and family and the madness that came with it, all through that prism of time.

Breath to him had become this free form dive down thirty meters, and the fight to the surface, desperate for that single cleansing breath of air, and

Life had changed for him, and drastically, simply sitting in a chair talking his arm clustered with IVs,

Moving his oxygen tubes across and around the bedstead, these took on the superhuman. We talked for as long as I could stand the room, and then I'd left, seeing his reflection as my own.

I planned to switch trains at Belmont to the Brown line and on to Southport, that millionaire's neighborhood where he lived with his wife for years.

Those fresh-faced women and men in the neon compartment reminded me of myself thirty years ago, going to work at advertising agencies downtown, and

Stopping off afterward for drinks: Riccardo's, Billy Goat, some seedy South Side jazz joint, or way up north on Broadway to the Green Mill for a final drink, absolutely the last.

Spending half the night on those unknown streets with revelers. Raucous and repentant.

They seemed so young, and so vacuous, with ears or eyes fixed to cellular screens.

We'd be reading the Tribune, or the Wall Street Journal, or making some inane comment about city politics. We knew people, or the people who did.

The train stopped before Fullerton Avenue, and as I glanced out the window I saw the same den window of the townhouse I'd lived in for years with my ex-wife and daughter.

Rush of memories flooded inside the stale compartment air. Those snowy Christmases, full-tabled candle lit Thanksgiving dinners, and the sultry summer barbecues surrounded cacophonous with friends and their children.

Subscription theatre tickets, and the overpriced champagne on New Year's. Café Bernard around the corner on Webster.

The Gallic himself at the table, nodding, "Madame," as she tasted his choucroute.

"No, I'm not going to see another Beckett play, thank you." Happy Days, who could blame her?

And this deluge continued to flood my mind like the Mississippi over its banks. Underwater.

Wednesday pork tacos at the empty Cocina Modernas under the train tracks, stocky cook-waitress, same order. Extra spicy. Broken dam of consciousness, this Book of Kells, this whole chronicle with each important and unimportant date entered

On that kitchen calendar. With the polar bear photos. Her flowery cursive... The frequent erasures. Yellow underscores, and those telltale smears.

That red brick and the black mansard roof. Reliving it all, each moment as it had happened. Do I live here? I've got to get off at the next station.

Suddenly there was a jolt as the train lurched forward, and in another flash it had all vanished. The next train stop was announced.

Stray Alley

When I figured that I'd become a marketable abstract painter in those later-in-life years when flip-flop decisions don't count for much anymore,

Living above the Raid Gallery in a Civic Opera rehearsal building, downtown, five minutes from Chinatown, right off the I-5

At the defunct Pabst Brewery with a few other decent painters and a catacomb of poseurs, sculptors of plastic limbs for horror films, and those facile mechanics of fire-spewing Sci-Fi robots. Roaming the alley at dusk. After stray cats.

There wasn't a place for anybody else's art in this sprawling town, no Caravaggio, Poussin, or even Monet prints had ever existed; nothing, everything a blank canvas.

You'd have to look elsewhere, to the movies. Cinema was the only thing that mattered. To those poster classics from Polanski's Knife in the Water to John Ford's black and white Panavision Stage Coach with a young John Wayne. Chinatown with Nicholson was OK, too. Maybe Giant.

Because in LA, you painted little stick men and women, all doing something, almost anything: screwing or killing each other, or robbing banks.

If you could come up with some kind of narrative, something you could animate maybe if you had to, then you had it. Everybody understood.

This moviola, every frame in constant motion. Predicted smiles.

Warmer Still Water

Why I went can somehow be explained, I'd been some time now in this unconnected limbo,

The answer had been to remain in this imposed repose, do little, hardly missing those few people we saw, which were mostly her friends, and

Because I had these equatorial friends of years before, I went to visit them, invited to stay there forever, to immigrate, and I flew to Rio.

What would I do after ten years in Brazil, a country I'd grown fond of in the past, though where I spoke almost no Portuguese?

How would I make any money? Try to resuscitate what I done in the past, hardly. Well, maybe that same absurdity.

When I checked into that commercial hotel in Leblon, it was with no real plans, perhaps rent an apartment in Ipanema if that were possible, and then wait.

For what? Some kind of middle age epiphany. I laughed at the hubris even

Talking about missionary work in the Amazon where a friend's parents were missionaries, though I certainly could have started with the Bay Area soup kitchens if I had that need for service, instead I retreated into myself, and turned down that stream of lunch and dinner invitations that came my way, not returning the telephone calls. It became a self-imposed sabotage.

This would never come to pass; I'd see to it.
I slept until noon, and then went onto the beach for an hour or two, and napped away the blistering afternoon,

And finally walked to the Copacabana cafes in the evening buying drinks and talking with the ladies of the night, those

Women had come to know me, and we laughed and talked about politics and passion, and this awful misery of loss.

I believed that I might love one of these women, it didn't matter who she was, and she told me that for me there would be no money, only this love to share.

She whispered to me, "I have a little black blood, does that matter to you?"

I remember laughing awkward at what she had said, and told her no, it meant nothing, her red hair and freckles texture to me. It didn't matter.

For weeks we lived inside this steamy Carioca wave until I knew there could be no end to it, and one day I left.

Outside these Dotted Lines

A bellowed salutation from his belly, deadly honest and self-deprecating, this Hindu, his thick hair hidden inside a black stocking cap,

Rapid movements of obvious intent, his muscled tattooed arms, tawny, arms and artisan fingers hustling a chili order out of the deserted cafe kitchen on an ordinary overcast Chicago morning; Café of artists.

Wood-kiln Japanese jars guard the emptiness. Blue ash. Zen and the Tao. Mandalas, Shiva, all seemingly absent

In this overheated restaurant. An unsmiling Slavic grandmother moves her blond granddaughter closer toward the chicken salad. Babushkas knotted. Smiles meander as the Oder does.

Round-faced child eats forkfuls with abandon. This withered woman nods, pleased. A ceiling fan circulates the stale air, pungent smells. baking,

Outside the Ravenswood line train clangs on worn tracks north toward Evanston. Lighted windows of anonymity. Search for solitude inside.

Drawing circles on a blank white page, filling them in with broad lead pencil.

Rumpled-sheet dreams. Sweaty nights. Vanished, or ever were. A mind.

To obliterate the obviousness, and abandon what you think you know. Between those machined thoughts.
Paint outside the lines, inside the consciousness.

Without a Destination

On the downtown San Francisco street corner waiting for the light to change I'd happen to glance at the woman in heels standing next to me,

She'd wormed her way through the small crowd to the curb, ready to race across lunchtime Sacramento Street,

From the sideward glance I'd noticed her straight blond hair, shiny in the bright light which I've always found attractive in women, and it prompted me to turn toward her; It was Mary.

She'd once managed my office complex, and we had liked each other, at least initially.

Everything I thought I'd wanted then. Trim, young, and smelling of violets and peppermint.

We'd even gone to New York for a long weekend, and whatever it had been that we had disappeared almost as soon as it had appeared.

Gotten involved right after my divorce, so much younger. Such a foolish thing to attempt, that had ended in particular heartache at the time,

This flashing memory of six years before had forced me to smile, and say. "It's wonderful to see you again."

She beamed back, and said, "I'm pregnant," and I had answered quickly, "That's great, you're married now."

"No, but I'm going to have a baby. The father's a chef, you've probably been in the restaurant." And she told me its name.

We walked across the crowded street with nothing more to say to each other. In that awkward silence,

Repeating, "It's so nice to see you," and half-heartedly waved, hurrying through the nearby Embarcadero arcade without a clear destination.

Only the same escape from myself.

Third Floor Front

That painting studio I had in Upstate New York, sat on the third floor above the movie theatre off the main street in Saugerties,

And after coffee from some alley bakery down the street with the restaurants, I'd sit and look at the Dallas Weiner's sign across the street, maybe stare at it for an hour,

Figuring I might be inside some lost Hopper canvas. All those same lines, the rendered wooden frame and brick buildings, this sadness, and even that Catskill sky became all these muted primaries, and as isolated as all his paintings.

I'd sit there, not distraught, but not pensive either, estranged to myself as all his interiors Walk in circles,
Sometimes moving charcoal on the newsprint I'd tack up on the wall. Nothing ever came of it.

Started on what I'd known, the West Coast, small canvases. Rectangles.

For weeks I painted hard-edged California pastels that smelled to me like LA, or what I'd remembered about Santa Monica,

Desperation and the pretense, the guy walking down the street with an inflatable wife, and the women in front of the Coffee Bean on Main Street, caressing the face-lift cuts behind each other's ears;

All essentially about nothing, or perhaps very little, a reductive effort about starting with a place, or a person,

And finally ending with the sound of ripped tape, and this otherwise meaningless confluence of straight lines.

Memory was only this transit ticket, the train seat next to the window, and the sound of masking tape on the scratchy gesso surface whose awful blankness reminded me of everything that I despised about myself, gradually became this redemption.

With red acrylic. The blood of some unrecognized Christ.

Marais

Twilight shadows this narrowed labyrinth of Victor Hugo's rapaciousness and his mistress' insouciance; the corridors of Juifs their rough-cut African diamonds and

Hasidic prayers, Barukh ata Adonai Elpheinu. Blessed are You, Lord Our God.

Whose serpentine trains of betrayed children and empty sandstone gargoyles haunt. Open mouthed. On those wet October streets.

Behold, these ghetto windows lit in darkness.

Hear me, Adonai.

It was here on the Paris streets in the soft rain I thought of another time, and wished for more.

Dollar at a Time

When I walked to work at the Embarcadero from the house on Lombard Street, I'd first go down the hill to Columbus Avenue in North Beach, maybe forty-five degrees steep,

Past Chinatown, Telegraph Hill in the distance, City Lights Bookstore, moving across Broadway traffic with reconstructed Carol Doda's breasts above.

Back alley Finocchio's. Boas and stiletto heels.

Onto the sidewalk passing Coppola's Zoetrope Studios into the Financial District; Fourteen minutes.

Each morning pleasant enough past the espresso and pastry smells from cafes, and in the evening the return to garlic aromas that filled the street.

Around dusk this destitute man my age, homeless though with clean clothes, a gentle face greets me with genuine smile;

He looks for me most days on Columbus because I don't see him as horrid, there's something likable about him,

We talk as we walk along the sidewalk, sports, the weather, the city. Even the president whom I dislike.

Over the next two or three months, I'd given him maybe ten bucks, dollar at a time.

Started to walk alongside me, talk about himself, and how he'd gotten to this. A Marine, and years before had a wife and a daughter.

Lived in the East Bay.

One morning, I'd seen him early enough to buy him a breakfast of croissants and coffee, and we talked. Conversation. Intelligent, polite.

Admitted he'd become a drunk, Ended anything decent. Lost a couple of jobs, and his wife left him. Never heard from them again.

I offered to drive him over to the VA hospital where they'd help him. Shook his head. Been in Swords and Plowshare.

They'd locked up a couple ex-Marines he'd known. Psycho wards. Padded cells.

Slept on these streets. Outside. These narrow doorways. And once a few months later, I'd seen him half drunk at a festival in Washington Square.

Staggering and disoriented. Several women had pushed him away when he pawed them trying to dance together. Finally, someone called the cops.

Something I couldn't ever change, and we'd avoid each other if our glances met on Columbus.

Then he disappeared completely from sight, probably lying in some Mission District gutter.

I'd mentioned him to my wife at dinner several times, and she'd shake her head, warning me, "Just don't tell him where we live, OK?"

When the Beginning Sadly Becomes the End

I had loved the San Francisco Press club when it had existed, because it doesn't anymore. It was a refuge from a dissolved marriage, and that aftermath.

Those days when it occupied that magnificent former Union League Club building on Post Street around the corner from the St. Francis Hotel, and

All the raucousness of Union Square in those last days of its life, before the plug was pulled and the vintage building was sold to pay its debts.

Someone had the idea to raise money for the deficit by emptying the attic of its fifty years of memorabilia and junk,

Unidentified boxes of useless items, someone had thought worth keeping, and had piled on top of another.

They called it an auction of the club's long history of Hearst newspapers which struck most of us as downright hilarious, the papers had disappeared, unimaginable cripples of print.

Someone had arranged for a Saturday afternoon in the upstairs bar where the Club secretary might try to sell a few of the items, to a handful of the members, and some of the unwary public who had wandered in, or a few friends.

Petting Benny Bufano's black cat sculpture perched on the bannister on their way up the stairs to the second floor.
I had taken a girlfriend with me to the auction, and she sat complacent as the beer mugs and parkas of another time were sold for a few bucks.

Suddenly when someone had pulled out a box of photographs she woke up, sitting erect, and laying her small hand on my wrist.

They held up a black and white press photograph of Bobby Kennedy. It was signed and it had been distributed to reporters the day he had opened his California campaign for president.

This little dark-haired woman nudged me, and I bid five bucks, which was the only bid, and became its proud owner.

She said to me, "Bobby Kennedy spoke around the corner in Union Square to a crowd that day. Before he came in here to talk to the press."

Her father, a psychology professor at SF State in those years had put this little girl on his shoulders in the crowd for her to see the next president.

As she whispered the story to me, I had smiled, and handed her the photograph, "It's yours."

She had it framed in her architectural studio at home the last time I saw it and her, for we couldn't find our common language of the heart.

That next day in 1968 in Los Angeles on his way to speak to a downtown hotel overflowing with supporters, Bobby Kennedy was shot dead in the kitchen corridor.

This happened not long after King was killed, and I had said to myself, "My God, when is this going to stop?"

It hasn't, won't. When this beginning becomes the end.

Before Eight o'clock Mass

A redundant face-slapping Chicago April rain insinuates its ever wet presence underneath flapping crosswalk umbrella skirts, sentenced to the harsh wind,

Those oh-so-wrong flat black shoes nearly drowned in this corner cigarette and candy wrapper gutter, as those anxious cars speed staccato, this con tempo,

Through automatic red light changes with those muscled left turns up Ashland before it's too late.

Heading home wherever that is, or going somewhere, almost anywhere on the cold Sunday morning, too early, even before eight o'clock mass, or even a first coffee.

Before this mythical flood. Of unsung granite-faced Jesuits with soft palms.

Horns blare, once, twice, three times, inside distracted drivers offer oaths to these overcast heavens through no-shatter windows and move rapidly into the narrow turn lane.

It's about time and motion, impatience, and hardly anything.

Sinai

McDonald's otherwise noisy restaurant waits mute in this numbed desert heat with brand new wrought iron outdoor furniture, saddened chamber

For these feasts whose date palm fronds shadow the blinding afternoon glare.

Sirocco sand scattered terrace cobblestones. Pharaoh's Egypt, tired Sinai of

Wadi's and automatic weapons. Coveted, this unlikely desire of terrorists, and broken oasis promises.

Once Jewish, though reason had surrendered, Arab
Sharm el Sheik, bejeweled scimitar of Bedouin tea sweetness on these thin parched lips as tourists walk these steamy brick promenades,
Seaside enclave for civil servants and foreigners.
Its embattled president himself watches bikini-clad Italian and Russian women, and those few hijabs in this warm sea.
Armies lurk in the darkness.
Under a desert sky.
Part this Red Sea.

Walking on Wet Streets

Continuous rattling cough, persistent, as something grey and
unseemly is spat on that dirty asphalt, a threadbare wool-sleeve arm
he wipes the unhappy mouth, now

Slowly moves from this sidewalk to the street, looking three blocks
west down Irving Park. Nothing.

Across the wide lines, Popeye's Chicken's red roof turns white.

A single police cruiser quickly passes, splashes the yellow painted
curb. Damn.

Number 80 to Lake Shore, and then angered step back into the
boxy glass bus shelter, anxious

Bereft with this interminable wait. Broken shoelaces from a circled
wagon train.

Pink bloodless fingers tighten around a steamy cardboard coffee cup
as

Chilled fetid breath and bittersweet bean aroma disappears into
moist air

Above these scarfed and pensioned men and fat women huddled
uncomfortably together on white rugs of fallen snow,

Their faces and smiles watching the wet city streets.

Try to Remember

When my daughter attended eighth grade and we lived in a Victorian red brick townhouse on Webster, every morning

She'd walk those two blocks to the elevated train taking it downtown next to the sprawling library and descend below the street to the waiting IC train and

Finally walking these three blocks to the university laboratory school. Thomas Dewey's icon to Socrates.

That whole year. I think she loved the independence then. Now this same journey strikes me as unthinkable. In a shooting gallery city of such monumental possibilities.

A place where I see the once street beauties of Bucharest, still made-up for a boulevard promenade, wrestle mops inside Yoga studios, the smile faded, and on the

Summery morning sunshine lights this room as if Thomas Hart Benton painted this same industrial Midwest in my own tired eyes,

And bitterness stains those parched lips, and this world surges onward, perhaps without resolution, or with some resolve so unimaginable as to escape any recognition.

Ten killings this past Sunday within four hours creeping into the hushed breaking warm dawn,

With this randomness that only human beings are capable of, without reason, or purpose, some awful surge of unspeakable evil, inexplicable even to those bent fingers on triggers.

And though she'll never ride that same train into or through those neighborhoods where these killings continue she instead drives her own daughter to another university tomorrow, and perhaps we've learned nothing from this.

Troubadour

Darryl Hannah and Neil Young made a feature film about the cultural dangers of your I-Phone, and they talked about high art,

Perhaps seriously, I don't know, and this fearful metronome, a relentless

Barrage of ubiquitous content, that linqua franca we've come to speak, and warned of the deluge of this absolute nothingness;

They wept for this, or rather for its absence.

An abbreviated line formed outside the Music Box theatre, cordoned off with dusty royal blue velvet ropes, quietly garrulous yet poised and rather polite,

Non-smokers, near-retired attorneys and advertising agency vice presidents, and of course those curious, all this coiffured greying;

So well spoken. Not pushing anyone for the slightest advantage.

These twenty middle-aged bodies seemed to be at parade, really, awaiting the rock troubadour and his movie star companion who'd soon grace the empty stage after the film, and then they'd know for certain if he'd aged gracefully.

Because most everyone in this casual snaked nighttime queue secretly hoped he had not.

Writ Large

Easter morning's reluctance glances with this unspoken and absent warm insouciance at carefully laid Victorian-hewn bricks of once certainty upon

These deserted streets of present mayors and baseball players and retired postmen; Voices heard within the subdued

Echoes of those footfalls sounded in a cathedral of men, whose yellow winged flowers hidden in their earthen crypt, interred still. All fast

Asleep, and as the breaking dawn's unrecognized silence and cold wind embraces me a startled tawny cottontail crosses the mottled sidewalk lawn, and I recall
Words

Writ large for rebirth and resurrection, this psalm an unexpected gift, drunk from Welch's grape juice.

Frangipani

A grey fragrant scent fingers its Malacca pathway into these lonely night hours, unobserved this elusive smoke. This wound corkscrew trail of Frangipani's whitened petal trapped forever in the orange flame, succulent and
Alone inside an empty sky,
This same remembrance, an
Aphrodisiac of all fulfillment:
Where has it gone?
Held tightly in this autumn smile, that same softness, whose
Sugared breath on icy front stoop of forgotten words once whispered into the disappeared winter mist. A silken cloud. Rising with
Warm wanton lips that sought this gentleness though only for the touch, and then at last transformed.

Refused Asylum

Once these womanly hands casual at outdoor café tables, espresso and croissants, porcelain cups steaming on silver trays, linen napkins, her Austrian filtered cigarettes, then;

Now prayer crossed, impoverished in this last asylum, her nails painted hemorrhage redness manicured and arthritic from a forced labor to survive,

This unmistaken Balkan siren, her teeth now broken and discolored: Who could find a dentist in that maelstrom? Her long wavy hair dyed a harsh metallic black, pulled back, the furtive glances. A gravelly voice, disconsolate.

Kosovo and Herzegovina. Murder and reprisals, and even more death.

This nation, devolved, into a primitive tribe. And madness.

Both sides, many sides. Ruthless and heavily armed,

Where the flags changed with the weather, your killer yesterday's friend,

There to see; she coughs with cheap cigarette breath, her smeared rouge on high cheekbones,

Listen. Few hear, and faces turn away.

The social worker from Thresholds comes and she tells him that her health isn't good, and finding a cleaning job is tough, one that pays over seventy-five dollars.

He looks at her more clinical than understanding the dark brown eyes, and quickly glances at the bling sound he heard on his cellular screen.

He's heard all this before.

Mazurkas

Prisms spotlight the few tarnished patina mouths open far above these modern articulated hybrid buses with their Matisse art exhibition and teenage safe sex posters,

Smokeless, uncomfortable, soulless, and perhaps even damned, democratic and

Over-crowded, without quarters or dimes on these too much traversed asphalt streets, now quieted without flashing police blue-lights and harsh night outcomes.

Across these broadly painted crosswalks march a directionless phalanx whose heavy-coat snow dustings bespeak the air's chill on this early April morning while Lake Michigan has yet to exhale its arctic breath, and where only the hardiest

Flowers dare to dance adagio to these windy mazurkas, so few in number with their daffodil innocence that confounds even the sun.

Piney Woods

Evening softness hesitates in brackish air, crying terns fly above off to the fecundity of muddy delta waters, and walking through this moist coastal air we stop as a young couple laughingly poses for wedding photographs alongside the Alabama city pier

Garrulous in their early twenties, she black complexioned, he, white, uncomfortable in this rented tuxedo starched collar chafing the muscled neck, this man appears

Even unusually pale, clean-shaven, so attentive to his chosen bride, while an eight-year-old black flower girl dances around them as a maypole, and in her purest innocence blesses what she sees, and the breaking

Waves of a once pristine New Spain bay wash under the wooden pier where few eyes of disdain, either white or black, or even faint surprise touch the excited couple as

A gentle wind blows toward an abandoned trench in the nearby piney woods where those last shots were fired from a dying slave state.

Boys and old men only with few bullets, to stave off what? It was the end for them, and how could they hold a line that didn't exist anymore, these last to perish for a cause lost from its beginning.

The black bride hugs the white groom in her enthusiasm, in her future, in her happiness of the moment, and of the hereafter, her husband now, the celebration noises echo from the open doors, laughing and joy.

Overpowering silence of this coming night finally reigns, and darkness slowly unfolds its eager fingers among the stars.

Sparrows

A small flock of common tan sparrows, quintessential forever of nature's brazen thieves frolic unfettered and innocent in clouds of dry dirt,

Foraging or is it playing, thrashing inside these flying mirages of a Sahara, perhaps

Rutting, but no, instead a spontaneous tryst with each solo performance and turn virtuoso,

These feathered actors joyous joined by more now from the dark green boulevard canopy, and then as quickly vanish into the dusk.

Trigger Finger

Afternoons of frantic metal grinds, undulating missteps back and forth at stop signs with bouncing tire melodies as

The cumbersome almost vacant blue and white CTA bus signals its wide turn across crowded Ashland onto Irving Park

Toward risen sweetness of major league baseball oaths locked inside summer's last chrysalis. The ballpark near.

Watch that rangy towering southpaw abandon this trampled mound at top of the fifth, shamed by those opposing bats.

His notorious fastball flaccid, those curves limp their way into the home plate dust and oblivion.

A three-run inning with one out, manager tobacco spat outside the dugout. Call for another beer in the stands, ten bucks.

Wait in the silence, this uncalled for armistice that pervades in this city of trigger madness. Forty-four shot over the weekend, eleven dead.

On a bungalow porch dusk's orange light illuminates a turning page, and the familiar cicada chorus sings of this coming night above a child's cry from an atoll though already drowned in these oceans of uncertainty.

Anonymous Rain

Punishing coastal rains unheralded, and then just as quickly dissipate in greenness, and the fall afternoon becomes pregnant with the brackish moisture of a gulf only miles away though its salt smell slowly disappears high above the cotton rows and bent collard greens as spotted cows low,

Nearby those retail malls offer what must be offered, takeout coffee, and the fried chicken thighs and breasts and wings, and colored t-shirts.

Feel the increased weight of this humidity on your bare skin almost scriptural as if it exposes your many sins so silently, anonymous,

Those of such a far distant past that they could only torment you and no one else, yet why seek forgiveness? To cleanse, to be free.

Born of youthful eagerness and later misplaced haste, ambition abandoned along the roadside,

This same path already on some parchment of heaven you can never read, ignored long after you on this spinning earth, smilingly added to those feathery dark clouds drifting in the hard evening rain.

And before sleep this now forgotten rain returns again, this time without warning, the comfort of its tapping rhythm on the skylight.

Unvarnished

The beliefs remain for many, these men across the table from me who grew up here, or somewhere along this southern coast, and though well-spoken for the most part, educated as formally as all of us, calm, and forthright,

You listen underneath their words for those hidden meanings, the riddles of ambiguous speech and suppressed emotion, the anger and resentment of a disappeared past, and you can see the momentary glimmer, the acceptance of this loss in their faces, their careful smiles, what their fathers held on to, or didn't in the end,

Grudging as it may be and the few words of regret that this, the present, the unvarnished, or imagined now, has changed without their hand, or concurrence. Something far larger than these few men.

They talk of New Orleans neighborhoods of Italian and Irish working-classes, those insular blocks in Algiers, Treme, Gentilly or somewhere else in that troubled once Gallic city as those blacks veered off course and then innocently or not wandered

Inside the unmarked boundaries to the jeers of boys all too unconcerned to recognize or even know this trajectory of the inexorable was afoot, and coming so very fast that it will and has gone careening beyond them.

Though only in those rare moments do they question that memory, this fleeting remembrance, and it's of the future they can comfortably speak, or even understand as the coastal sun scalds the black metal café table. And everyone rises, smiling, a wave, a word to part with.

The time has come for their air-conditioned cars to take them into those nearby gated communities, and only a painful history will make note of what was said and done in this place before them, one hundred and fifty years ago when the sabers were lowered.
A black man laughs loudly in the parking lot, they slow, and smile.

Summer of a Very Small Discontent

The church, or you might call it a regally adorned chapel, built when this town claimed another country, or soon would, and where the Louisville and Nashville railhead skirts the river's edge of a grassy village that saw laughing men in grey tunics marching that July,

Vestments of the Church of England came only twenty years before, this once unsettled wilderness, resplendent with pale linen and silver chalice, this unspoken scripture, those Psalms whispered.

A daughter married in this church on a hot June afternoon when the yellow sunlight races unchecked through the stained glass windows of St. James forming these irreproachable muted reds, this spilled blood of Christ, found once among the fields of the dying.

The bride in grandmother's lace waits anxiously in a penumbra glow as the organ notes call out to the stilled pine forest in their rich tremolo voices. Mockingbirds listen.

I walk her along those creaking slatted oak aisles, her soft birdlike hand on my dark suited arm, and commend her glorious spirit to another man who stands ready at her side, now

She lives her life without him, the summer of discontent.

Crumbling Ramparts

Carved forever on this dark granite headstone the chiseled words count and precede the name of this man interred below assumed to be Swedish, or maybe even Norwegian, or perhaps a seagoing Dane, those Vikings of greater myths, and

Since they all have kings and queens, and a few princes and princesses whom you'd occasionally see scandalously divorced in the back pages of Newsweek or even Time,

Smiling men and women you didn't know existed until your eyes saw the rather strange names, those elegant unpronounceable surnames of the arctic.

They were usually named Karen, Maria, or even Christina, and perhaps the manly Sven or an inquisitive Oleg,

And you remembered Danny Kaye dancing furiously across the silver screen in Hans Christian Andersen, heels in the air with the Tivoli lights shining in the blowing snow behind him.

Now blinded by the glare of this early autumn Alabama sun, this once nobleman in repose beneath the blackest of stones, untroubled by that awful darkness of Ibsen's adulteries and suicides, or Strindberg's alcoholism and ruin whose words echo for eternity into the aurora borealis above those crumbling Lapland rock ramparts of loss.

Uncharted heavens of this Southern Cross, the same blood moon whose Aquarius sky portends the Venus silent whispers, now fill this darkness, those human doubts and agonies, written large in the unnamed constellations, and breathe the brackish incense of this Gulf wind deep into your lungs, heat of its red dirt, the touch of its caressing palms, and magnificent nothingness.

Alto Saxophone Notes

I hadn't turned twenty-one yet that summer in New Orleans and I'd roam the French Quarter nights with enough for a beer maybe, one,

And as I walked across Canal Street back into the narrow streets there was a line of teenagers, the oldest

Sixteen, wrapping around the corner from this empty elementary school auditorium, the front doors splayed because of the early Spring Louisiana heat, stage lights blaring bright. A performance.

Fifteen or twenty boys in this serpentine line around the deserted street corner, all holding brass horns it seemed, mostly saxophones but a few trumpets too,

The horns in one hand and reeds or chrome mouthpieces in the other, all quiet and tense, not talking with the boy in front or behind, lost

Inside their musical world, some humming and others tapping fingers on clean blue jeans, almost all black faces,

Except for one who was gangly and pasty white. He held a black enamel clarinet, his finger gentle on its neck, poised.

The schoolhouse doors were slung wide open as I slid into one of the auditorium back seats, and for twenty minutes heard the auditions,

Too melodious and full of discovery and melancholy enough to describe with words, from these almost children who knew they'd become jazzmen, this tortuous path set before them, all ready to embark on,

And after that, I drank the single beer I could afford with some half-broken down guitar player at a Quarter strip club who told me when he was really drunk, almost falling down,

He'd go to this potter's field cemetery not far from the edge of the Quarter where eighty years of musicians lay in mostly unmarked graves, or below scattered chipped stones,

And toward the dawn he swore you could hear some of them play in the hot night, guitar strings and wailing alto sax in that humid thick bayou air.

Undisciplined Pelicans Fly South

A feathery caravan through the wispy clouds was ragged at best, not the sort of unflawed precision you might see with the black and grey

Canadian Geese in their tight formation moving toward those icy clear Ontario lakes, hovering undaunted above the thick verdant firs of Minnesota,

No, not quite that same impressionist canvas, instead you dreamed that moment

Of a weary battle scarred 1917 morning whose blue skies filled with the garish colored fabric icons and humming engines of British and German aircraft,

All in those maddening dog fights to somehow protect those fetid and dying trenches of this graveyard No Man's Land, the carnage of the wholly unimaginable.

Behold these pelicans so awkward, undisciplined, the fifty or even hundred birds above that windy Gulf waters moving in a continuous broken line,

Birds in and out of some uneasy randomness like the ragged Lafayette Escadrille planes before them,

Moving like a beehive into the heavens until, of a sudden, they became this single line of utter resolve, and fly quickly across the lagoon surface, and it reminded

Me of my long dead grandfather who had been in that Great War where he had lost a brother in France and another at Gallipoli whose souls took flight into those darkened skies.

He had only ever become airborne in an open two-seater at some Pennsylvania country fair as perhaps a dare from the other miners holding their half-drunk beers,

And how this day so very many years later his never to be known great-grandson at seventeen pulls those metal and rubber wheels of his small Cessna into the welcoming slotted belly and heads alone into the blowing clouds above a meandering muddy Mississippi. His mother watches, concerned, while the boy soars, freed.

I hear the plane's engine in the clouds above unseen, his small aircraft alone in that bright blue vastness.

Night Talk

Nighttime sorely abandoned in this humid fall sky whose broad moon only half grown to its fullness watches a wanton Mars.

Whisper siren sonnets across those celestial distances to her lover's empty obsidian embrace, and this lonely star beckons, calls forth, but is it heard? Hold me, come, she calls.

Below we marvel at this too perfect conjunct of its mighty interstellar geometry, seen boldly above people and things being mortal and therefore insignificant

And within insignificance we discover something greater, something unnamed that draws us, slowly and steadily,

Toward this unspoken longing and then plunging at last into those leagues of the human heart where the treasure of fulfillment lies unclaimed.

From your silence what must we know? These winds build against my waiting face, and I reached for the soft feminine hand next to mine, and learn the language of the harrowing night.

Unwelcome

Tiny birds of mid-summer came to the porch joyously in song and also silence, and with such fierce instinct forge this sculptural monument.

It prospered as they did with the fecundity only God permits creatures. I watched them nurture and feed these scarlet finch fledglings, flitting as busy parents are wont to do, until all fly away.

But then, new tenants came without much announcement or ado, and made those few changes they thought needed,
the occasional twig added or taken away or bent more gently to caress the fragile eggs, and so,

Life continued and early one morning sharp beaks again appear, and the world became the place for the song trilled into the warming morning sun, and I too felt the caress on my face,

Though lastly, sadly two fledglings fell out, and to their deaths, while others perhaps soared, or we hoped,

And we saw with horror, though nature has this balance we fear to question, that last unwelcome tenant, its dark awful eyes looking off into some void, this coiled snake who found its way down from the roof shingles onto the wooden porch column and into this nest of tranquility.

Oh nature of rightness, speak to us.

Born and raised in the eastern Pennsylvania coal regions, Colbert served as a wartime Navy Seabee, then went on to extensive travel. A television and stage actor, filmmaker and author of eleven books of fiction and poetry, he lives in Coastal Alabama and is working on a Civil War novel.

www.ingramcontent.com/pod-product-compliance
Lightning Source LLC
Chambersburg PA
CBHW020947090426
42736CB00010B/1301